coolcareers.com

New Media and Multimedia Producer

Barry Mazor

the rosen publishing group's
rosen central
new york

For my parents, Bettye and Joel Mazor, who know something about combining art and organization.

Published in 2000 by The Rosen Publishing Group, Inc.
29 East 21st Street, New York, NY 10010

First Edition

Library of Congress Cataloging-In-Publication Data

Mazor, Barry.
  New media & multimedia producer/ Barry Mazor.
     p. cm. —(Coolcareers.com)
  Includes bibliographical references and index.
  Summary: Describes the various types of jobs available in the field of   new media development and the education and training required.
    ISBN 0-8239-3102-1
   1. Mass media—Technological innovations—Vocational guidance—Juvenile literature. 2. Interactive multimedia—Vocational guidance—Juvenile literature. [1. Mass media—Vocational guidance. 2. Computer science—Vocational guidance. 3. Vocational guidance.] I. Title: New media and multimedia developer. II. Title. III. Series.

  P96T42 M375 2000
  302.23'024—dc21
                                    99-045519

Manufactured in the United States of America

CONTENTS

ABOUT
THIS BOOK

Technology is changing all the time. Just a few years ago, hardly anyone who wasn't a hardcore technogeek had heard of the Internet or the World Wide Web. Computers and modems were way slower and less powerful. If you said "dot com," no one would have any idea what you meant. Hard to imagine, isn't it?

It is also hard to imagine how much more change and growth is possible in the world of technology. People who work in the field are busy imagining, planning, and working toward the future, but even they can't be sure how computers and the Internet will look and function by the time you are ready to start your career. This book is intended to give you an idea of what is out there now so that you can think about what interests you and how to find out more about it.

One thing is clear: Computer-related occupations will continue to increase in number and variety. The demand for qualified workers in these extremely cool fields is increasing all the time. So if you want to get a head start on the competition, or if you just like to fool around with computers, read on!

chapter one

WHAT IS NEW MEDIA?

Since you've picked up this book, odds are that you already know that enjoying today's new media as a consumer is pretty cool. Whether you realized it or not, you have probably used or at least seen some of the key kinds of new media.

Put simply, media are means of communication. Old types of media include newspapers, television, radio, and magazines. New media, however, include:

- Interactive multimedia CD-ROMs or the newer DVD-ROMs, loaded with information or entertainment, that let you click and get a response to your questions
- The coolest video, audio, and graphic interactive Web sites

- The 3-D graphic designs and animations seen in everything from computer games and Saturday morning cartoons to the most amazing special-effects sequences in major movies
- Multimedia "where to" and "how to" information kiosks or stands found in stores, hotels, airports, and museums
- Totally new media that use television, cable, satellite boxes, game platforms such as Nintendo and Sony PlayStation, wireless phones and other communication devices, the World Wide Web, computer software, handheld personal digital assistants (PDAs), and even the good old printed page, *together,* and in endless new combinations. These combinations are just beginning to appear, but they are limited only by the imaginations of the creative people who build them—and by the consumers' interest in owning and using all of them! Often, though, when consumers are asked about their interest in these new media products, the answer is "I'll take one of each!" So the nearly limitless field of new media offers an exciting future for anyone who is considering working in it.

We're talking about new games. New kinds of movies. Live, interactive video that "streams" over the Internet to your computer. Making your classroom into an exciting new place.

Could there be a cooler high-tech career than one in which your job is to think up, build, operate, and bring to people the most cut-ting-edge information and entertainment avail-able—every day?

Probably not! And new media producers are working at these

Could there be a cooler high-tech career?

"cool-as-you-can-imagine" jobs right now, and will be needed to deliver more shiny, new, challenging, and exciting prod-ucts for years to come.

Since this area is wide open to new possibilities—and, as you'll soon see, always changing—you are going to need to get a handle on what the field is like right this minute, what working in it is really like, and where it is going. Computer-related fields in general, and the new media design field in particular, change faster all the time. Without a crystal ball, no one can be sure exactly what "new media" will be by the time you have finished school and begun to work. If your interest is not simply in using exciting new media products but involves finding a cool career producing these products, this book will give you a glimpse of what lies ahead.

WHAT ARE WE REALLY TALKING ABOUT? ▶▶▶▶▶▶▶▶

One thing all forms of new media have in common is that they are made using computer software—digital tools that create, use, mix, and organize the information and entertainment they hold. Often, what these media hold is a mixture of both information and entertainment. For that reason, new media professionals often use terms like "infotainment" or more simply, just plain "content."

New media producers are people who make and provide various kinds of content using digital tools. These digital tools, which include software programs and hardware (such as digital cameras, recording equipment, and so on), are used to create all new media and content.

The action of thinking up and delivering projects is now generally referred to as "authoring" new media, since words such as "writing," "taping," "drawing," and even "designing" don't exactly describe this new activity. Authoring involves everything from writing digital computer codes and programming that allows specific projects to work to using technical software, to setting up the way that different elements in the media will work with each other in the final product.

Authoring itself is a kind of interactive process between the producer and the tools that he or she uses, so in some ways, making new media has a lot in common with the experience of using it. The content delivered through new media of all types is also becoming more and more interactive.

The word "interactive" is used often, but rarely does anybody stop to consider what it really means. Interactive new media is not designed to be read and forgotten or to wash over you, couch-potato style. Instead, the user asks for and gets things from the medium and content, responds to it, plays with it, personalizes it, and becomes involved with it. The user does all of this live—or in computer talk, "in real time." (Notice that we don't call the new media user a "reader" or "viewer" or "player" or "the audience." Each of those terms only describes one of the many aspects of participating in interactive new media.)

One other important point: The interactivity of new media is not limited to that between the user and the software. It may also take place in the form of new kinds of interactive communication between real people, with the content and media designed to make that interaction easier or better as an experience. Graphic-aided chat rooms with cartoon characters who stand in for you are one example.

New media producers constantly look for new ways to interest consumers—and keep interesting them— by making new kinds of content more powerfully interactive than ever before.

New media producers are people who make and provide various kinds of content using digital tools.

You might think that people with job titles as different as Web page designer, game creator, and educational CD-ROM author would work at very different kinds of companies. But that's not as true as it once was, because similar tools and skills are now used in all of these positions. Today, new media production companies and new media divisions at larger companies, schools, and agencies all tend to cross those lines.

One firm that does all kinds of new media production is 415 Productions, based in San Francisco, home of many new media production companies in a neighborhood known as "Multimedia Gulch." The 415 team produces new media for many of the best-known high technology companies in

San Francisco and the nearby Silicon Valley area. Some of the media they produce include:

- Live multimedia auditorium presentations for the digital imaging software company Adobe, and new media authoring software company Macromedia
- Computer animation for the introduction of a new Apple computer
- Web site design and handling for San Francisco's famed Fairmount Hotel
- A CD-ROM explaining the complex opera plots for the San Francisco Opera.

With new media firms working on such varied projects, the job possibilities become more varied at each company.

WHAT AWAITS YOU ►►►►►►►►►►

It probably would not be a surprise to hear that many people are interested in new media production, so there's quite a bit of competition within the field.

With technology so advanced and fast-moving that whole new types of technology are being invented every year, the new media field looks a bit like the new frontier environments in *Tomb Raider,* into which Lara Croft leaps and tumbles—full of unpredictable turns and possibilities.

People who work in the field now find their work that fast-changing, competitive, and engaging. But—so far, at least—there have been no reports of new media producers being shredded by a T. Rex!

There are ways to prepare for the competitive new media environment, as there are for Lara's in *Tomb Raider*, such as showing up with the right tools. And as with adventure games, picking up a few hints about what lies ahead can't hurt either. We're going to look at what new media production entails, what the industry needs and expects from newcomers to the field, and what tools you're likely to need to work there. Since we are talking about cool careers here, there will also be some good news about a key question that you probably have about this new field: "Who will get to play in this new field?" There's a good chance that it could be you.

Lara Croft of *Tomb Raider*

chapter two

NEW MEDIA: TO HERE AND FROM HERE

As you read this, new media has already been "new" for a long time. But it is changing and evolving all the time, with some old opportunities tossed to the side as brand-new ones arise. The reason we know that you can expect the unexpected in both the direction of media technologies and in the sorts of jobs that involve working with them is that we have already seen so many surprises.

In the late 1980s, there were brand-new new media jobs, too. These were most often known as multimedia producer jobs. The term "multimedia" put the spotlight on combining the kinds of media that already existed—and they were very different from the ones that you and I might have today. That late-1980s producer put together presentations with sight, sound, and text for educational purposes or

perhaps for a business sales pitch. The media put together would have included analog (not digital) video clips stored on foot-wide laser disks. The clips would have been arranged for projection in a confer-ence or schoolroom, used with desktop publishing tools (for changing the look of text and graphics), and put on photographic slides. There might have been some recorded music arranged and sequenced coming from audiocassette tapes. All of that automating and sequencing might have been done with some not very user-friendly software for a PC or Macintosh (or even the Amiga, which is no longer available), on computers with less power and memory than you would find in a pocket electronic address book today. But even with limited power, the develop-ment of the presentation of the text and video on big screens got things moving and created new jobs.

Five years ago, the world was multimedia-mad, but the excitement then was about the CD-ROM. Many new media jobs from that time are still with us. They involve coming up with ideas; working with digital photos, video, and graphics;

and the process that was, and still is, called authoring.

You might think that things have calmed down since those early days—that is, until you realize that back then the new media field didn't yet involve the Internet and World Wide Web! It wasn't long after the CD-ROM became the symbol of new media that the Web was invented. The Web was able to handle all sorts of multimedia. Internet access became easier, and people who get paid to predict things began predicting that soon, phone companies, television networks, and computer companies would all offer multimedia products. These products would include text and video and audio, interactive games and soap operas and grocery shopping—all on your television, which would replace your computer. You'll notice that none of this has actually happened—at least so far.

Still, you can see that change has to be expected along this career path. The experience of Jane Jensen provides a good example of this. Jensen, a creative author of interactive games, is famous in the new media world. Among other episodic adventures she has created for both game discs and graphic novels is the Gabriel Knight occult mystery series. *Gabriel Knight 1* came out in 1993 and featured a clever story set in New Orleans. It used simple two-dimensional (2-D) graphics that might look pretty crude to you today. By the time the second installment was released three years later, Jensen was able to use interactive "click and fetch" video, and live actors had taken the place of the 2-D graphics. In episode three, released in 1999, the action is highly interactive, and the look is mainly photorealistic 3-D graphics.

Looking ahead, in her creator's diary on the Web, Jane Jensen suggests that because fast-action arcade games have been selling so much better than adventure games like hers, the best medium for *Gabriel Knight 4* might be virtual-reality theaters. Of course, we don't quite have those yet! But this new media creator has not only continued to make the products she wants through all of these technological and taste changes, she has been able to adapt to the changes. We might even say that she's rolled with the punches just like Lara Croft (who is not one of Jensen's creations, by the way).

Right now, new media companies are on the verge of introducing interactive video actors. These characters will be as programmable and interactively controllable as graphic characters today, but they will look like real people in a video or film because their skin will be digitally imaged from real video, not graphics. Maybe the face will even be the player's own.

We're seeing children's toys that combine computer games with real-world robot characters that you can have

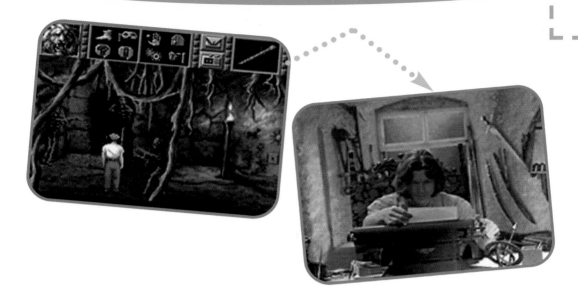

right there in your living room. We've started to see on-screen instructional CD-ROMs and videos that you use with your real-world microscope. And soon we'll see boxes that sit on top of TV sets that are linked to the World Wide Web and can play DVD discs. These set-top boxes will allow players to store winning games that they have played, even if they've played them against an opponent on the other side of the world. You'll also be able to store your photos using the same set-top box.

Companies have begun to make game stations with video- and information-handling capability, allowing not only for more complex interactive games but also for functions that you're used to doing with your computer. Soon there may be video or graphic story episodes and lessons that you can download to your Palm Pilot or other personal digital assistant—or to your two-way video phone that will have a sharp new high-resolution screen. We're seeing Web sites like Broadcast.com and The Den offering old and new movies and videos that you can download whenever you like.

Sound engineers use MIDI programs and computers to make music.

And then there's rock singer David Bowie. Bowie recently decided to create his next single by recording it during a live World Wide Web "cybercast" in which Web viewers could watch the whole session in the form of a walk-around-in-the-scene, see-it-from-all-sides video—live, as it took place.

With an exciting array of new media such as these just arriving on the scene, we won't know for sure which ones will be winners or losers, passing fads or lasting new media additions you might work with in the future. But we can be sure that creative people will try to make the most of them.

chapter three

JUST WHAT IS A NEW MEDIA JOB?

You are probably wondering right about now: Is this new media producing career really a computer programming "techie" job, or is it a job in the arts? And the answer is . . . yes!

Talk to enough people doing this work for a living (as you should if you're interested in this field as a career, of course) and you'll hear one thing over and over: Their jobs involve both technical and artistic skills. And they're glad it's like that.

From the most complex computer programming side of making new media projects to the most artistic design and script-writing parts of the work that depend on a different kind of imagination, authoring now amounts to real interaction between the producer and the working tools available to do the job.

Not long ago, a pretty firm grasp of computer programming and a fair amount of college and post-college schooling were practical necessities for any job involving the creation of new media. To use the tools, you had to have the education.

Even today, in a field in which the availability of tools and imaginative use of them are still key for everybody's work, the technical and the artistic can't be separated completely.

But not everybody needs know how to make the artist's brush, or how to build the engine in the car they'll drive! Authoring tools have become more powerful and in many ways more simple. Many of them now come ready to be put to work on a project. That ease of use is changing jobs—who does them, how, and even where they are done.

At most new-media production sites— whether at companies dedicated to new-media production alone or at larger organizations that have new-media departments— you will find people working on what is called "higher level" programming.

That means more basic, nuts-and-bolts programming, heavy on math. These programmers use the most current computer tools. A quick look at the computer section of your local bookstore will display today's preferred programming languages. Right now those include C++, Java, HTML, Visual Basic, and more, but the languages change rapidly and frequently.

This sort of new media programmer does need special training, in college and often beyond. There are likely to be jobs that demand knowledge of the latest in programming for some time to come. Individual companies will often have a number of people working with high-level programming tools to create an original way of approaching new media. Programmers create sets of programming tools that new-media authors can use and reuse in their media. These tool sets are usually referred to today as "engines"—a pretty descriptive term, really, since they are the power behind the projects.

If a programmer creates a way to make swarms of animated characters (or spacecraft or buzzing dragonflies) change direction on command, for example, the production company can apply that "animation engine" or "game engine" more than once. In some cases, large software firms even sell those engines as set-up tools for more general use.

Engines put computing power in the hands of the game maker who is not a traditional programmer. This also means that anybody who handles the most technical aspects of programming will now work day-to-day with others who design backgrounds, characters, or other types of content for projects. They will also work with people who sell the project, and, in many cases, those who arrange

A quick look at the computer section of your local bookstore will display today's preferred programming languages.

the use of photos, films, music, and text for that project. Nobody in new media gets to hunch over his or her computer alone forever! It's the sort of career where individuals bring different strengths and interests to a team. People involved in the writing, designing, and selling parts of new media production still need to be comfortable and familiar with the technical side, and vice versa, to know what is possible and what's not and at what cost.

We should make one point right now: If you have been thinking that the people doing the math part must be the guys and those doing the art part are the girls, think again! This field is wide open for all types of talent, whomever it comes from. As just one example: 415 Productions, which we discussed earlier, is headed by a woman computer scientist from Oxford University and a man who started out as a filmmaker.

PROJECT PRODUCTION: WHEN IMAGINATION MEETS THE TOOLS

New media writers and designers meet with businesses, nonprofit organizations, or other clients to get key ideas about what a project needs and what the intended audience may want from it. Knowing and understanding the technical and content "inventory," or the tools the producer can readily put to work, is certainly important in cases like that. Not so obvious is knowing what the technical and content options are or could be. Making the best use of these options is how the new media artist's imagination gets to play.

Recently, available tools met available imagination and content at hand in new media after the movie *Titanic* was such a success. A number of new media companies happened to have the same idea: "Hey, let's do a CD-ROM about the *Titanic*." There were many new media products created to cash in on *Titanic*-mania, just as there were numerous books and documentaries about it. Some well-known new media products show how imagination, tools, content, and sales techniques were brought together at different companies.

- *Titanic: Adventure Out of Time* from Davidson & Associates/GTE Entertainment was a popular PC and Mac game. The player was a passenger who could tour the ship, interview a variety of people on board, and uncover secrets that would allow him or her to get off the wreck alive or even save the *Titanic.* Many who scrambled on board this detailed, graphics-based rendering of the ship found that when they saw the movie, they already knew what was on the other side of the doors before the film's characters went through them! Game owners could also download characters from the maker's Web site to add to the game. The company had used the same style of action in the earlier game, *Dust,* so the tools for producing this style were already available. That was important for deciding the style of the *Titanic* game.

- *Robert D. Ballard's Titanic: Challenge of Discovery,* produced by Panasonic Interactive Media, used this explorer's famous undersea video of the remains of

This realistic-looking scene from the movie *Titanic* was done with computer animatition.

the *Titanic.* By using video that contained special information that had been collected on underwater expeditions, the producers created a game that let players pilot their own expeditions to the site of the wreck and take their own pictures. As a bonus, the game also featured other famous shipwrecks that could be explored. Here, the availability of the video material helped determine how the programmers would approach the authoring of the CD-ROM.

🖱 *Total Titanic: A Night to Remember*. Andromeda Software obtained the rights to use *A Night to Remember*, a movie and book about the sinking of the *Titanic*. They put that material on CD-ROM, along with a blueprint of the ship, biographies of people who had been onboard, and comments by experts. The producers then added a search engine that allows the user to find a topic in these documents and jump right to the point in the movie where that particular topic comes up.

James Cameron's Titanic Explorer. To make this CD-ROM, Fox Interactive and Cameron, director of the 1998 movie *Titanic*, used the massive amounts of research and model-making that went into making of the movie, ready to be applied here in a new way. What did they do, besides simply showing a lot of pictures of Leonardo DiCaprio and Kate Winslet? They packed in around 800 of the original photos they had used in making the film, along with the full text of American and British court inquiries after the sinking of the actual ship, blueprints of the ship, and a detailed graphic simulation of the ship's final hours. It is not surprising that such a simulation would be available. After all, much of Cameron's *Titanic* movie was actually output from banks of computers at the digital effects company Discrete Logic.

You can see how the different styles of these projects, and even what they turned out to be, were shaped by the technology and material available, and by the fact that to sell, each product had to have something special that would grab people's attention.

Each product was also shaped by the talents of the people who created it. These tasks—coming up with an idea, coming up with the way to create it, and then making it all happen using the right tools—are the ones on which people in new media careers spend most of their time at work. How individual tasks are assigned depends very much on the size of the new media production unit and the resources it has at hand.

chapter four

WHO DOES WHAT, AND WHERE

When most people imagine what producers of interactive games or Web sites or audiovisual learning materials are like, they probably picture gangs of twentysomethings in tiny, brand-new companies in San Francisco or New York. They imagine these whiz kids performing rocket science while sending out for pizzas on-line and waiting for their big break on the stock market. Is that a realistic picture? Well . . . nothing says you have to live in New York or San Francisco!

Even if many people who work in this field are relatively young, not all (or even most) new media jobs are in brand-new start-up companies, either.

More and more, people are creating new media for organizations such as hospitals, schools, city agencies, or divisions of chain stores, on-line sales organizations, newspapers, or magazines. All of these companies have new media needs. Their departments may vary in size, but the best places to see the full range of new media production are naturally in the largest production sites. These also include new media units at some of the biggest traditional media firms (movie and TV production, publishing, and so forth) and the biggest computer-age media companies.

DOING IT LARGE: MICROSOFT'S INTERACTIVE MEDIA GROUP ▶▶▶▶

There's no better example of a big media company than the new media unit set up at software giant Microsoft. Interactive Media Group (IMG) develops important software and other products that you probably know. These include:

- http://www.msn.com sites on the Web

- The Gaming Zone, responsible for interactive games such as *Flight Simulator* and *Age of Empires*

- CD-ROM and DVD-ROM multimedia products like Works, Greetings Workshop, Picture-It, and Home Publishing

- Encarta multimedia encyclopedia products

Jim Cox, lead product planner for Encarta at Microsoft, is in a good position to describe what new media work is really like. His main tasks as planner are to decide what direction to take with a product, how to make its content most useful, and what features need to be changed or improved. Jim also makes sure everyone on the team is headed in the same direction. He works with a wide range of people and has a good view of each individual's job.

The Encarta group makes the *Encarta Encyclopedia*, the *Encarta Interactive World Atlas,* and the new *Encarta World English Dictionary.* The Encarta encyclopedia includes the well-known version for CD-ROM, as well as a somewhat different version for the Web and separate versions for different parts of the world—American English, British English, French, German, Spanish, Dutch, Italian, Portuguese, Swedish, and Japanese—with different encyclopedia content for each, depending on local interests. The encyclopedia contains 42,000 subjects, with

Bill Gates of Microsoft

over 16,000 multimedia pieces—graphics, photos, sound, animations, charts, maps, and video.

Jim Cox reports that there are more than fifty content editors working on Encarta projects, each focusing on a particular subject area—science, geography, and so on. These editors continue to follow the news carefully to decide what new topics the encyclopedia needs and when older ones should be updated. Editors find experts to write the articles, then work on the text that the experts submit to ensure that it is accurate, up-to-date, understandable, balanced, and interesting.

In book publishing, this would be most of the process. But since this is new media, getting and editing text is just the beginning. Now the editor has to decide what multimedia should go into this new article.

"For a long and important article like [the one on] evolution," Jim says, "the editor might request over fifty pieces of media—an illustration of a DNA strand, a picture of Charles Darwin, a table of key archeological finds by date, or a map showing key sites."

At this point, a second group of editors, called media acquisitions editors, look through collections of images and sounds to find the best ones available. Encarta doesn't own all of those photos and video clips, so the editors must get permission from the owners to use them and pay for them.

This process is called licensing.

Now the media production team takes over. They scan and size tens of thousands of images. Images are scanned at a number of sizes so that they can be used in different layouts. Media production staff must also compress the images—making the file sizes smaller—so that they fit on the CD-ROM or DVD-ROM. Then they add closed captioning to all video and audio clips for those who can't or don't want to hear the audio parts. Production workers write captions for every piece of media. A team of indexers creates an index of the final text, so users can search it by hot links and keywords.

Now editors get to work on those important interactive elements. The Encarta features editor might decide that the best way to explain how a lever works would be through an interactive presentation in which the user can operate an on-screen lever and see the results. The editor, a graphic

designer, and the multimedia author get together and

discuss the details of this presentation. They decide what it should show and how to make it work using text, audio, stills, and animation. Graphic designers are responsible for the overall look of Encarta. They design the layout of each article, choose the text fonts (the way the type looks on the page) and the colors, and they create the introductory screens that you see when you first open the encyclopedia.

"But that," Jim says, "is still only half the battle. Now we have to get all that content organized and put it together into a piece of working software. A lot of other teams work on this part of the project." There is still much more to do— that math part, for instance! The actual programming is done by software development engineers, also called developers. Some work on the tools needed to create and store all of that content. Others work on the *Encarta Encyclopedia* itself, writing programming code for about two-thirds of the year and then "debugging" it (fixing all of those pesky problems all software is prone to) for the last third of the year. Software engineers called testers (or "people who like to break things," as Jim Cox calls them) have the job of catching bugs and thinking up new, extreme ways to test Encarta. This is all done to make the encyclopedia reliable when it is ready for customers to buy.

A program manager (PM) is the hands-on boss of each individual project. The PM makes the schedule after figuring out how much work will be put into an Encarta version and how much time it will take given the number of people avail-able. When all the bugs are fixed, it's the PM and the lead

tester who must be satisfied with the quality of the fin-ished product. They are the ones who officially decide when to release, or ship, the product.

At that point, as Jim describes it, "It's time for the mar-keters to take over—the ones who try to sell our products to you." The marketing team determines the price of the prod-uct, creates the packaging that you see in stores, and tells the world all about how good the final product is. They place advertising, talk with the press, and do many other things to get the word out. None of the creative work matters if no one knows that a new media product is available!

Where, you may be wondering, did all of those people—the editors and production staff and PMs and marketers—come from? What did they need to know to get these jobs? Jim Cox says, "There are a few jobs around here where most people have had very specific training and experience. The developers and testers have all studied computer science and programming. The designers have all been to school to study graphic design. Most marketers and planners have been to business school or done marketing at other companies before Microsoft.

"But there are lots of jobs that don't really require specific backgrounds. The editors, for example, have a wide variety of experience and skills. Some have been teachers, artists, or librarians; some are in their first jobs after college. Some media producers have worked in television or the movies, and many have studied Web design and development."

For Jim, the coolest aspect of this work is thinking up and designing new media features for Encarta that make full use of the newest media. "A few years ago, we saw the technology that allows a user to spin around in and see all of a 360-degree panoramic photograph. We knew that we could use that as an effective teacher! And we designed a new Encarta feature called *Virtual Tours*. You can visit Mount Everest or Alcatraz or Paris—places that you might not ever get to visit—and see all around. We created a map of these sites so you can always see where you are and which way you are looking. We try to come up with something new—something that is very cool and very useful—for every version of Encarta."

Jim Cox himself earned degrees in electrical engineering, computer science, and English before starting at Encarta, which helps when working with people with varied backgrounds that cross the lines between science and art. And he actually designed communications satellites, so he really is one of those creative "new media rocket scientists."

Work on Encarta has changed with its success, Jim reminds us. "When I started on Encarta several years ago, the team was a lot smaller. On a small team, people have to do several different jobs to get the project done." That's the way things are at most new media production companies.

MIDSIZED COMPANIES►►►►

There are many midsized, specialized new media production companies, and in many places. They usually work on producing new media for companies and organizations that have a need for new media but can't or don't want to do the work in-house.

Human Code, a company based in Austin, Texas, is a good example. It's dedicated to creating a broad range of new media projects for companies and organizations. Human Code handles about twenty to thirty projects a year. Their work has included everything from the Jump Start animated multimedia math discs for grade school kids, to CD-ROM presentations that helped sell Compaq computers, to the *Lost Civilizations* CD-ROM produced for Time-Life, to the *Barbie Riding Club* game, to writing computer codes that help a TV station's newscasts to be turned into streaming video for their Web site. All that, and they create "smart" toys—interactive, computer-powered toys—too!

The award-winning new media producers at Human Code have jobs focused on design, 3-D animation, and programming for the Web. In fact, they work on all of the functions we have discussed. "Writers, musicians, artists, coordinators, producers, architects, designers, educators, book readers, storytellers, set designers, and database builders are all welcome and have fun applying their skills to multimedia here," says Courtney Tucker, a senior producer at Human Code. She's currently producing the CD-ROM *Redbeard's Pirate Quest* for Zowie Intertainment and the Jump Start Fourth Grade *Mystery of the Mine Monster*. That involves a lot of hands-on work at a medium-sized firm like Human Code.

How did Courtney get into this type of work? She worked in animation and TV production in California before returning to her home in Austin and finding this exciting job in her own backyard. "I love working in such a flexible and creative environment," she says. She likes the fact that the interaction between small teams of workers is needed all the time, and that people work on a variety of different tasks, so that job descriptions are less strict than they would be at a larger company. As cool as working on such interesting projects surely is, Courtney mentions a different aspect of the job that is the coolest for her: "Working with all of these talented and intelligent people, making really cool and fun cutting-edge creations is exciting. Problem-solving with them is also part of the fun." Interacting with the team beats interacting with the projects for this new media producer, and she suggests that preparing to work that way might be the most important training for the job.

Courtney emphasizes that to work up close and personal on a team every day, you will especially need "to learn how to work with all types of people, with all types of skill sets, to tap into those people effectively." She also offers this advice: "Learn how to pay attention to details, to be a good listener . . . so you can hear what someone

New media designers help create "smart" (interactive, computer-powered) toys too!

is asking for and figure out a way that you can deliver more with creativity and ingenuity—on time and on budget and having fun in the process!"

SMALL BUT POWERFUL▶▶▶▶

It's also possible, even in a small new media outfit, to do some very hands-on new media production work and to have a positive impact on your community and your neighbors. A good example of a firm that does that is Web Hed Technologies, a Web design and hosting firm based in San Antonio, Texas.

With a small but very involved team, this little company has attracted much attention. They have brought a local food manufacturer, Toudouze Market, on-line, selling 6,000 items on the Internet and in the process creating many jobs in a neighborhood that needs them. The people at Web Hed have helped to train local underprivileged kids in computer technology and have even hired some of those kids to work at the company. They've hosted and operated the local public TV station's Web server; built a Web site for the Texas Interagency Council on Early Childhood, which helps families with small children with disabilities; and even developed a Web site for Primarily Primates, a sort of rest home for chimps who have been retired after being used in research projects.

None of this was accomplished with good intentions alone, however. Web Hed is currently run by a dynamic young leader (and young mother), Janie Martinez-Gonzalez, who brought business and community knowledge to what was once an even smaller team. She has built Web Hed into a successful business while doing good in the community.

"Because we are minority-owned," Janie says, "we feel that it's our responsibility to help the underprivileged, especially those who don't have the same [computer] access opportunities."

Like Courtney Tucker of Human Code, Janie Martinez-Gonzalez also finds interacting with people the coolest part of her work. "I love the interaction that takes place. I get to meet some interesting individuals with great work history. Sometimes I even meet individuals that are difficult to work with, but I love the challenge! My staff get to do what they love and do best on a daily basis. Hard work is fun if you like what you do—and we do!"

chapter five

WHAT YOU CAN DO NOW

You may live in a place where forward-looking companies are searching for young interns. Or you may go to a school that offers many in-school technology opportunities.

Or maybe not! Fortunately, there are various kinds of software—for example, software for making multimedia Web pages the easy way—available everywhere for those who are interested. There are handbooks in your school and public library on Web design. Service organizations in your neighborhood may offer more tools for learning about computers and multimedia than you have access to yourself. There may be people affiliated with these organizations that are working in new media and can be resources for you. There's no substitute for getting involved with real projects and real people, to find out which parts of the process most appeal to you and suit you best. Meanwhile, you'll be gathering the tools—just the way Lara Croft would— to enter the new surroundings up the road.

Organizations in your area may offer tools for learning about computers and multimedia.

A bit of Ms. Croft's inventiveness and attitude couldn't hurt either. Consider the case of teenager Shawn Brenneman, for example. Shawn was called up on stage at a computer show a few years ago because he could already use MetaTools' new program Kai's Photo Soap so well. He was soon being called the "Doogie Howser of digital imaging"—and working as a demonstrator himself!

Or what about Brent Sims's and John Taylor's movie, made with a camera attached to a Nintendo Gameboy, which cost a total of $100 to make? That movie has won awards and taught big-time effects makers a thing or two! When people want to make new media, they find a way. That's what careers in new media are really all about. And that's really pretty cool.

WORDS.COM: GLOSSARY

authoring Creating new media. Authoring may include writing software programs, finding and editing images, or writing and editing text.

content The text, graphics, video, audio, and other elements that make up a new media product.

graphics Illustrations, photographs, and other images

HTML Hyptertext Markup Language, a programming language used to create many World Wide Web sites.

imaging Creating, editing, and manipulating graphics.

interactive Involving the user; requiring active participation from the user.

media Means of communication. Traditional media include newspapers, television, and magazines; new media include CD-ROMs, DVD-ROMs, interactive games, and other things that take advantage of computer technology.

multimedia Products that combine more than one type of communication; for example, CD-ROMs that include video, photographs, sound, and text.

software Computer programs that allow users to perform specific tasks.

tool-set A group of software and computer programs that allow users to create content.

RESOURCES.COM: WEB SITES

You can learn more about the field of new media and multimedia production at these Web sites.

AGORA Digirati
http://www.digirati.com

Apple Multimedia Program (AMP)
http://www.amp.apple.com

Boston College—Careers in Multimedia
http://www.bc.edu/bc_org/svp/carct/multimedia.html

Center for Electronic Art
http://www2.cea.edu

Creativity Café
http://www.creativity.net

Design Authoring Technology—Crafting Multimedia Titles
http://www.mindspring.com/~markarend/dat

desktopPublishing.com
http://www.desktoppublishing.com

Digital and Multimedia Commentary Online
http://moliere.byu.edu/digital/index.html

Index to Multimedia Information Sources
http://viswiz.gmd.de/MultimediaInfo

International Interactive Communications Society
http://www.iics.org

Márcio's ToolBook & Multimedia Hotlist
http://www.inet.com.br/~mhavila/toolbook/index.shtml.en

MediaLab
http://www.media.mit.edu

Multimedia Authoring Web
http://www.mcli.dist.maricop.edu/authoring

SIGGRAPH
http://www.siggraph.org

Women in Computer Visual Arts, Effects, and Animation
http://www.animation.org/women

BOOKS.COM: FOR FURTHER READING

Baker, Christopher W. *Let There Be Life! Animating with the Computer.* New York: Walker Publishing Company, 1997.

Cohen, Mark H. *New Media for Kids.* New York: Market Focus Publications, 1997.

Coorough, Calleen. *Getting Started with Multimedia.* Fort Worth, TX: Harcourt Brace College Publishers, 1998.

Leonard, David C., and Patrick M. Dillon. *Multimedia and the Web from A to Z.* Phoenix, AZ: Oryx Press, 1998.

Peck, David D. *Pocket Guide to Multimedia.* Albany, NY: Delmar Publishers, 1998.

Peter Collin Publishing Staff. *Dictionary of Multimedia.* Kinderhook, NY: i.b.d., Limited, 1998.

Rathbone, Andy. *Multimedia and CD-ROMs for Dummies.* Indianapolis, IN: IDG Books Worldwide, 1997.

Weigant, Chris. *Choosing a Career in Computers.* New York: Rosen Publishing Group, 1996.

INDEX

CREDITS

ABOUT THE AUTHOR

Barry Mazor has been a radio news reporter, disc jockey, and music reviewer and has written for television, the movies, and high technology and business publications. He has produced, edited, and directed films, and worked for film studios and television production companies. He has a Masters of Fine Arts from the Tisch Graduate School of Film & Television at New York University. Since 1988, as Editor-in-Chief of Film & Television of *Advanced Imaging* magazine, a trade publication for developers and implementers of digital imaging systems, he has tracked the birth and growth of the multimedia industry and technology.

ACKNOWLEDGMENTS

The author thanks all of the new media and multimedia professionals, quoted and unquoted in these pages, who willingly described the work they do in enough colorful detail to make this book possible.

Photo Credits: Cover photo © Superstock; pp. 7, 14, 22, 42 by Thaddeus Harden; p. 10 by KarenTom; pp. 18, 38 © CORBIS/Jim Sugar Photography; p. 20 © FPG/Arthur Tilley; p. 30 © CORBIS/Judy Griesedieck; p. 32 © David Stover; p. 34 © CORBIS/Roger Ressmeyer; p. 40 by Shalhevet Moshe.

Design and Layout: Annie O'Donnell

Consulting Editor: Amy Haugesag